Forgiveness Made Easy

3rd Edition

Dag Heward-Mills

Parchment House

FORGIVENESS MADE EASY (3RD EDITION)

Copyright © 1998 Dag Heward-Mills

3rd Edition Published by Parchment House 2022
1st Printing 2022

Find out more about Dag Heward-Mills
Healing Jesus Campaign
Write to: evangelist@daghewardmills.org
Website: www.daghewardmills.org
Facebook: Dag Heward-Mills
Twitter: @EvangelistDag

ISBN: 978-1-64330-525-7

Contents

CHAPTER 1

Christian Forgiveness

And that ye put on the NEW MAN...

Let all bitterness, and wrath, and anger, and clamour, and evil speaking, be put away from you, with all malice: And be ye kind one to another, tenderhearted, forgiving one another, even as God for Christ's sake hath forgiven you.

Ephesians 4:24, 31-32

The Bible tells us that when we are born again, we become "new men", or "new creatures".

When a man becomes a doctor or an army officer, he is expected to behave in a certain way. In the same way, a certain pattern of behaviour is expected of anyone who claims to be a Christian or a "new man".

One of the primary qualities of a new man is that he forgives. The new man should not live in unforgiveness.

According to biblical principles, the new man must not live his life according to what goes on in this world. In the world, people hardly forgive. It is natural for a person not to forgive, but to seek revenge. However, when you become a new man, God expects you to forgive.

Indeed, one cardinal difference between the Christian and the unbeliever is that the Christian has the ability to forgive and release the offender.

A new man must be able to forgive!

I know that I am a young man, and I know that I have not seen all there is to see in this life. However, in my short life I have experienced many wounds and hurts. I have also come to learn that learning to forgive is essential in moving along with God.

There are times I have stood in my pulpit claiming not to have a grudge against anyone while deep down, my heart was full of hurt. This is true for many, many Christians.

In my daily walk with Jesus, God has shown me how to be free from this syndrome of hurts and wounds. Indeed, the Bible makes it clear that offences shall surely come (Matthew 18:7). But how can I expect God's forgiveness if I will not forgive?

I hope this book will be a blessing to you.

Let us obey the Lord and receive His blessing.

CHAPTER 2

The Lord's Prayer Test

After this manner therefore pray ye: Our Father which art in heaven, Hallowed be thy name. Thy kingdom come. Thy will be done in earth, as it is in heaven.

Give us this day our daily bread.

AND FORGIVE US OUR DEBTS, AS WE FORGIVE OUR DEBTORS.

And lead us not into temptation, but deliver us from evil: For thine is the kingdom, and the power, and the glory, for ever. Amen.

Matthew 6:9-13

Now, how can you be sure that you have forgiven somebody? Often, we say, "I have forgiven. I have nothing in my heart against him." However, you will find that there is still a grudge you bear somewhere in your heart.

As a pastor, I have stood in the pulpit and said that I had nothing against anybody. But in reality, I had something against someone. I thought that I had forgiven the person. Unknowingly, I had not. Later into the year, I realized that I really hadn't forgiven this person.

Through my search of the Scriptures, the Lord showed me what I call "The Lord's Prayer test". This is a test to prove whether you have truly forgiven your offenders.

The Test

Pray The Lord's Prayer: keep praying. When you get to the point where you refer to those who trespass against you, specifically mention the name of the person who offended you. It is important to specifically mention the name of that person.

So the prayer becomes for example, "...And forgive me for my trespasses, as I forgive Araba Lucy." In other words, "If I have not forgiven Araba Lucy for her sins against me, please do not forgive me!!!"

If you are able to pray like that, asking God to forgive you specifically in relation to your forgiveness of certain people in your life, it is very likely that you have forgiven them. However, if you cannot mention the person by name in this prayer, then you have not forgiven them!

Think of that man who promised to marry you. You waited for him for six years. But he deceived you and ruined your life. Remember, you need to forgive even him. Insert his name into The Lord's Prayer, to see whether you have really forgiven him.

Apply The Lord's Prayer test to every ugly or unpleasant situation you have ever encountered. This will help you to determine whether you have truly forgiven the person, because you need to do so!

CHAPTER 3

Unforgiveness Makes You A Wicked Servant

But the same servant went out, and found one of his fellowservants, which owed him an hundred pence: and he laid hands on him, and took him by the throat, saying, Pay me that thou owest. And his fellowservant fell down at his feet, and besought him, saying, Have patience with me, and I will pay thee all.

And he would not: but went and cast him into prison, till he should pay the debt. So when his fellowservants saw what was done, they were very sorry, and came and told unto their lord all that was done.

Then his lord, after that he had called him, said unto him, O thou wicked servant, I forgave thee all that debt, because thou desiredst me: Shouldest not thou also have had compassion on thy fellowservant, even as I had pity on thee?

Matthew 18:28-33

Unforgiveness makes you a wicked servant in the eyes of God. Often, even as born again Christians, we find it difficult to forgive, because we least expect that certain people will hurt us.

Sometimes best friends become worst enemies. Yes, even husbands and wives can become sworn enemies. The closest person who told you he loved and cared for you, can become your worst enemy.

As Christians, we need to remember that God has forgiven us for lots of horrible things. Do not allow unforgiveness in your heart to make you a wicked servant in the eyes of God.

19 Billion Versus 6 Thousand

To illustrate this, Jesus told the parable of the unforgiving servant. He compared the Kingdom of God to a certain King who wanted to settle accounts with all his servants. One servant owed him 10,000 talents. When he was unable to pay, the King thought of selling him, his wife, children and all his property, but the servant begged for mercy.

The servant therefore fell down, and worshipped him, saying, Lord, have patience with me, and I will pay thee all. Then the lord of that servant was moved with compassion, and loosed him, and forgave him the debt.
Matthew 18:26-27

However, this same servant found a fellow servant who owed him just 100 pence. and immediately all hell broke loose. Despite his cry for mercy, the unforgiving servant threw his fellow servant into prison, till he settled all his debts. This was reported to the King.

Then his lord, after that he had called him, said unto him, O thou wicked servant, I forgave thee all that debt, because thou desiredst me: Shouldest not thou also have had compassion on thy fellowservant, even as I had pity on thee?

And his lord was wroth, AND DELIVERED HIM TO THE TORMENTORS, TILL HE SHOULD PAY ALL THAT WAS DUE UNTO HIM.

So likewise shall my heavenly Father do also unto you, if ye from your hearts forgive not every one his brother their trespasses.

Matthew 18: 32-35

Talents could be either gold or silver talents. One gold talent is worth approximately 1,908,587 US dollars. 1,000 gold talents are worth 660 million US dollars today. Therefore 10,000 gold talents is approximately 19 billion US dollars (US$19,085,873,400). That is the amount that this young servant owed his master.

God has forgiven us 19 billion US dollars and we are required to forgive our friends a few cents.

Perhaps, you think that you were not a bad person, even as an unbeliever. Maybe you were not a diamond thief or a drug pusher, so you think this does not apply in your case. It applies to everyone who has been a sinner before. Without raising a finger or uttering a word, every man's heart is utterly wicked.

The heart is deceitful above all things, and desperately wicked: who can know it?

Jeremiah 17:9

Sometimes, in talking about what somebody has done to us, we forget that we have also wronged God and man before. From God's point of view, a Christian who cannot forgive is rather strange.

God will forgive you if you murder, lie, fornicate, commit adultery, and practise witchcraft. However, God will not forgive you if you bear someone a grudge. That is the point at which God stops forgiving you.

7

And when ye stand praying, forgive, if ye have ought against any: that your Father also which is in heaven may forgive you your trespasses.

Mark 11:25

If you have an unforgiving nature, the implications are far-reaching. It indicates that perhaps you are not a "new man", or that you are just a pretending Christian. Over the years, I have come to see and believe that unforgiveness is one sin that God will not forgive. It may be for you the difference between life and death. Moreover, the sin of unforgiveness is to me, even more dangerous than the sin of fornication.

Often, because unforgiveness is not seen physically, many Christians feel that they can get away with it. But it is deadly if it is left unchecked in your heart. God will not hear your prayer, and He will not prosper or bless you if unforgiveness lingers in your life.

God will be angry with you, because He forgave you, but you would not forgive others! Remember, the Bible tells us the Lord was wroth with His servant for not forgiving. In addition, the Bible says the man who did not forgive his brother was handed over to the tormentors. Many Christians do not know why they are being tormented in this life. It could be because of unforgiveness.

Many times, we commit the same sins over and over again. Then we come to God expecting Him to forgive us. God looks at our numerous sins and says, "Okay, I have forgiven you." However, we come back with the same sin repeatedly and God has to forgive us. Now, if we refuse to forgive our brothers in the same way, do you not think that God will be angry with us?

Do not allow God to see you as a wicked person. Do not allow God to think that you are an unforgiving and wicked servant. That will bring about a curse into your life!

CHAPTER 4

Signs of Lingering Unforgiveness

And forgive us our debts, as we forgive our debtors.

Matthew 6:12

S ometimes unforgiveness lingers on and on, even long after the offence has been committed. People even bear grudges against dead relatives and enemies. It is a dangerous condition!

What are the signs of lingering unforgiveness?

1. BITTERNESS IS A SIGN OF LINGERING UNFORGIVENESS.

Let all BITTERNESS, and wrath, and anger, and clamour, and evil speaking, be put away from you, with all malice: And be ye kind one to another, tenderhearted, forgiving one another, even as God for Christ's sake hath forgiven you.

Ephesians 4:31-32

"Bitterness" can be defined as "degenerated unforgiveness". I define bitterness as a "long-standing degenerated unforgiveness".

The word "degenerate" is defined as "to pass into a worse state than one which is considered normal or desirable". Thus, when a situation passes from one stage to a worse state, it can be described as degeneration. Unforgiveness which stays in your heart for a long period of time, degenerates into bitterness. The cardinal sign of bitterness is that it begins to poison other people. The Bible cautions that when bitterness is permitted, it will spill over and defile others.

Looking diligently lest any man fail of the grace of God; lest any root of bitterness springing up trouble you, and thereby many be defiled;

Hebrews 12:15

I know some people who are so filled with hatred for their wives, husbands, mothers, fathers, or other relatives. A good example of a bitter person is a woman who has been hurt by a man.

The story line is often similar: The man approached you and told you, "I love you honey. You are the sweetest lady I've ever known, and I want to love you. When I saw you, my heart moved from the left to the right. I want you to know that if you were on the other side of the Mediterranean, I would swim across just to bring you some ice cream!"

Perhaps he also said, "There is only one pebble I see whenever I walk on the beach and THAT IS YOU!" You believed it when he told you he had seen many ladies, but that you were different. What you didn't know was that he had other pebbles on the beach, and that he had told other ladies these same stories.

You were a virgin and wanted to remain so until you got married, but he convinced you to give in to him, with the promise that he would marry you anyway. So he began sleeping with you. You did things you never dreamt of doing with your body. In fact, you also had to commit several abortions because you were not ready for babies.

Then, one day, he lets out the bomb that he cannot marry you after all. So many suitors wanted to marry you at the prime of your youth, but you refused them because of this "sweet talker". After you turned thirty-eight, most men shied away from you.

Now, you bear this man a grudge. You begin to hate him. Soon, you begin to hate him with a passion. With time, you have come to hate all men. You could not forgive that man, so you have lumped all men into this category. Your hurt has become a long-standing degenerated type of unforgiveness—bitterness.

Sometimes, such people begin to champion women's causes out of bitterness. They may remain unmarried for the rest of their lives. It can even develop further into sexual perversion. Sexual perverts are sometimes bitter people; bitter against those who perhaps hurt them sometime in their lives.

I remember a London taxi driver, who told me of his experience. Because of this experience he had vowed never to marry. He once had a live-in girlfriend whom he looked after. He took her to school, paid her fees, fed her and gave her everything she wanted for years. If she wanted anything, all she needed to do was to ask. She was almost like a wife. Then at a point, he began to suspect her of infidelity.

So one day, he told her that he was going on a business trip and would return after a week. To be certain that she would believe his story, he asked her to see him off. He went to the Kings Cross train station in London with her, got on a train and waved goodbye to her. However, at the next stop he got down, took another train and returned into town.

He did not go straight back home, but went to a drinking pub to while away the time till two a.m. Then he went home. When he climbed upstairs and entered the bedroom, here was his "girlfriend-wife", in his bed with another man. Both of them were stark naked in his bed. He threw her out of his flat, naked, and called the police.

After this experience he decided never to get married or to trust any woman. He could not forgive that girl, and he had now extended it to all other women. When such hurt degenerates into hatred, it is bitterness! Beware of becoming bitter after bad experiences! When a bitter person speaks, it affects, influences and poisons others.

Dear friend, as you read this, ask yourself: "Am I bitter?"

2. WRATH IS A SIGN OF LINGERING UNFORGIVENESS.

Let all bitterness, and WRATH, and anger, and clamour, and evil speaking, be put away from you, with all malice: And be ye kind one to another, tenderhearted, forgiving one another, even as God for Christ's sake hath forgiven you.

Ephesians 4:31-32

"Wrath" can also be defined as "extreme anger". One sign of the presence of extreme anger is that the person begins to act "wild".

Once, a man was so angry that he threw all the lunch that had been set before him at the wall. Afterwards, when tempers had cooled down, he had to struggle to clean the stained wall (anger really makes you do some foolish things)!

Extreme anger or wrath is a sign of lingering unforgiveness.

3. ANGER IS A SIGN OF LINGERING UNFORGIVENESS.

Let all bitterness, and wrath, and ANGER, and clamour, and evil speaking, be put away from you, with all malice: And be ye kind one to another, tenderhearted, forgiving one another, even as God for Christ's sake hath forgiven you.

Ephesians 4:31-32

The dictionary defines "anger" as "a strong feeling of hostility and displeasure".

I remember one lady came with her husband to the church office. Her husband said something which was not exactly complimentary about his wife. She exploded. The hostility was so glaring, and her behaviour was so bad that her husband rebuked her, "Is this the way to talk? Don't you respect the pastor?" he asked her. Then I sensed that the strong feelings of hostility between the husband and the wife were because of unforgiveness.

If you have this strong feeling of hostility whenever you see someone who once offended you, then there is some unforgiveness lingering in your heart.

4. CLAMOUR IS A SIGN OF LINGERING UNFORGIVENESS.

Let all bitterness, and wrath, and anger, and CLAMOUR, and evil speaking, be put away from you, with all malice: And be ye kind one to another, tenderhearted, forgiving one another, even as God for Christ's sake hath forgiven you.

Ephesians 4:31-32

13

The dictionary defines "clamour" as "loud abusive language, and loud demands or protests". How can you come to church so nicely dressed, looking so sweet and holy, and then go home and quarrel everyday with everyone? If your next-door neighbour decides to record the string of loud abuses, everyone would be surprised at your behaviour.

I believe that a Christian should not be loud and abusive in any circumstance. Clamour or loud abusive language is a sign of lingering unforgiveness. I know of a Christian church where there was so much disharmony that the pastors fought openly in church. They shouted at each other, and even used tear gas on each other. What a disgrace!

5. SLANDER IS A SIGN OF LINGERING UNFORGIVENESS.

Let all bitterness and wrath and anger and clamor and SLANDER be put away from you, along with all malice.

Ephesians 4:31 (NASB)

To "slander" is "to say bad things about someone, or to backbite".

When someone slanders another person, usually what is said about that person is false. Those who slander, often have the intention of destroying another person. People who slander their spouses must be watched very carefully. Slanderous people are often full of bitterness. There may be genuine complaints. But when it is continuous, then such a spouse has a deep-seated problem of unforgiveness.

A husband once complained to me, "Pastor, my wife is very wicked. In fact, she is a witch! If you have ever seen a witch before, you'll know what I'm talking about."

Take particular notice of people who say negative things to bring others down. I have heard pastors speak carelessly and negatively about other ministers. Sometimes these are people with whom they claim to have a good relationship. I take particular notice of such ministers. Most slanderers are filled with unforgiveness and bitterness.

From my own experience, I have come to know that, "He who talks to you about others will talk to others about you."

6. MALICE IS A SIGN OF LINGERING UNFORGIVENESS.

Let all bitterness, and wrath, and anger, and clamour, and evil speaking, be put away from you, with all MALICE: And be ye kind one to another, tenderhearted, forgiving one another, even as God for Christ's sake hath forgiven you.

Ephesians 4:31-32

According to Ephesians 4:31, one of the signs of unforgiveness is malice. "Malice" according to the dictionary means, "a desire to harm others".

I have encountered people who simply have a desire to hurt me.

The desire to harm others shows you that you haven't forgiven the offender. When you have truly forgiven, you won't desire to harm the person. Do you think God desires to harm you? Can you imagine what would happen to you if ever God should decide to harm you?

Malice backfires; spite boomerangs.

Proverbs 26:27 (MSG)

If you are a wife and you have a secret desire to harm or punish your husband, then that is malice. Sometimes wives punish their husbands by denying them sex. Some women cannot "commit love" with their husbands because of something they did. I have heard some women complain, "I can't bring myself to take off my clothes and do this with him. I'll go crazy if I have to sleep with him again." Once you feel this way, you have not forgiven.

15

One way you can tell that you have not forgiven, is when you feel uncomfortable at the mention of the offender's name. At the point when you can say, "Lord, I let him go," or "God will take care of it," then malice is gone. When you curse the offender, wish him ill or plan how to hurt him, then malice is still lingering.

You might complain and wonder why people hurt you so often. That is not the point! God expects us to forgive. Malice must go away!

CHAPTER 5

How to Make
Forgiveness Easy

For consider him that endured such contradiction
of sinners against himself, lest ye be wearied and
faint in your minds.

Hebrews 12:3

W hy Is It So Difficult for People to Forgive? Often, hurting people find it difficult to forgive because they cannot believe that the offender was the same person they trusted so much. This could explain the unwillingness of some spouses to forgive when their husbands or wives cheat on them.

Sometimes the emotional pain one goes through is almost unbearable, and as human beings it is not easy to forget. Though you may find it difficult to forgive, what God is saying to you is that it is very important to forgive no matter how traumatic the pain may be.

I want to share with you five steps that will make forgiveness easier for you.

1. ANALYSE THE OFFENDER AND THAT WILL HELP YOU TO FORGIVE.

Then said Jesus, Father, forgive them; for they know not what they do. And they parted his raiment, and cast lots.

Luke 23:34

There is the need to analyse the offender very well — that is, the person who did whatever to hurt you. Luke 23:34 gives an example of Jesus analysing the offenders. He said, "Father, forgive them; for they know not what they do."

As the people were killing and destroying Him, Jesus looked at them and said, "Father, forgive them." Jesus was not just forgiving them Himself. He had gone a step further, and was asking someone else to forgive them for the evil that they had done to Him.

The Son of God explained why they needed to be forgiven: because "they know not what they do."

If you analyse the offender, you will realize that although he is doing evil, he may not be fully aware of the implications of his action. As soon as you analyse it this way, it will help you relate well with whoever offends you.

I remember when one of my junior pastors was extremely rude to me. This pastor spoke in a way he should never have spoken to me. He shouted and threatened me. I was sitting with one of my senior associate pastors.

As this was going on, I looked at him and I said to myself, "He does not know what he is doing."

As he continued displaying and behaving in an unbecoming manner, I said to myself, "I am very sure he doesn't know what he is doing. Maybe he is confused or disturbed."

Later on, my associate said he thought I would dismiss him immediately, because the junior pastor's behaviour was appalling. However, I made the excuse for him that he did not know what he was doing or he would not have behaved in this way.

Learn to make excuses for people. Jesus made excuses for His own murderers! Perhaps your offender is sick, ignorant or confused.

If you are able to analyse those who offend you in this way, you will be able to forgive them. By analysing in this way, you will find that you have the capacity within you to forgive. It helps you to understand why a person behaves in a particular way. Otherwise, you can never forgive.

2. ANALYSE YOUR PAST SINS AND THAT WILL HELP YOU TO FORGIVE.

Brethren, if a man be overtaken in a fault, ye which are spiritual, restore such an one in the spirit of meekness; CONSIDERING THYSELF, lest thou also be tempted.

Galatians 6:1

When you analyse your past sins, you will not be so hasty to judge anybody. This is because you might have done the same thing (or something worse) before. Probably, you might have acted in the same way if you had been confronted with the same issue.

Galatians 6:1 cautions: "Brethren, if a man be overtaken in a fault, ye which are spiritual, restore such an one in the spirit of meekness; considering thyself, lest thou also be tempted." When you consider yourself, you will be more willing to forgive. When you think about your past sins, you will realize that you are not any better.

Some people who felt they were "holier" brought a woman to Jesus who had been caught in adultery. They wanted to punish her by stoning her. Jesus, who understood this principle of analysing people's past, asked for any man who had not sinned to throw the first stone. No one dared throw a stone because they all knew they had past sins (John 8:1-11).

When you consider your own self, you will not be so hasty to judge other people. As a born-again believer, you should be forgiving, especially when unbelievers offend you. Just remember what you did as an unbeliever. If it had not been for Christ, perhaps you would have done worse things.

Jesus said, "Father, forgive [the unbelievers] for they know not what they do." So analyse your past when you find it difficult to forgive your neighbour.

3. ANALYSE THE OUTCOME AND THAT WILL HELP YOU TO FORGIVE.

Joseph forgave his brothers when he analysed the outcome.

Now therefore be not grieved, nor angry with yourselves, that ye sold me hither: for God did send me before you to preserve life.

For these two years hath the famine been in the land: and yet there are five years, in the which there shall neither be earing nor harvest.

20

And God sent me before you to preserve you a posterity in the earth, and to save your lives by a great deliverance.

So now it was not you that sent me hither, but God: and he hath made me a father to Pharaoh, and lord of all his house, and a ruler throughout all the land of Egypt.

Genesis 45:5-8

Out of jealousy and hatred, Joseph's brothers sold him into slavery. After thirty years, God raised him from prison to become the Prime Minister of Egypt. Unaware of his new identity, his brothers came to him for help during a severe famine. Later, Joseph revealed himself to them. With remorse, they fell down and begged him to be merciful to them.

Sometimes, when you analyse the way things have turned out, or the way things are going to turn out, you can easily forgive. I remember that years ago when I founded my church as a young medical student, I invited a pastor from one of the great charismatic churches in Ghana, to come to my church and minister.

This man of God who had been preaching and encouraging us in my little fellowship at the university for many months, sent a message to me that, he would not "sow amongst thorns". Upon starting a church, I had suddenly been rejected by a man of God I highly respected.

So I asked myself, "When did we become 'thorns'?" He had been preaching in my fellowship of "thorns" for many months! I was very surprised, because I thought then, that he was my friend. Instead, he rather influenced my associate to leave me and the church. This almost broke up our baby church. He then told my associate to be careful not to associate with someone who was not "called of God".

This departure of my immediate assistant generated all sorts of problems among my own church members, who now began

21

to analyse me; whether I was "called of God" or not. That was not the only trial. I was also under fire everywhere. Some of my classmates in the medical school called me names, as I carried the church drums and instruments to and from the church.

"Why should you start a church? Who are you? Who do you think you are?" they asked me.

When I was going to get married, my parents-in-law went to see a certain pastor to ask to use his church facilities for our wedding. Our church did not have a church building then. The pastor told them that he would allow us to use his church only on the condition that we close down our church. He actually wanted me to shut down my ministry as a condition to use their facility. I had no friends anymore!

I remember inviting all the pastors I knew to my wedding. Believe it or not — no one showed up. When pastors were called to take photographs with the bridal train, there were none. I was completely rejected. It was as though I was evil. People just threw me away for starting a new church. At a point I felt like committing suicide.

Now, I realize that the Lord wanted me to be independent of man's help and praise. The Lord wanted me to stand on my own, go through the pains that I had to go through, and rise up to bear a particular fruit in His kingdom. Today, the "small rejected" church has expanded not only in Ghana, but has branches all over the world. It worked!

Recently, I saw some of these people who rejected me and I told them exactly what Joseph said to his brothers: "You meant it for evil but God turned it out for good." God knows that I don't bear them any grudge. These people are all my friends today, because God has helped me to forgive them. When you look at the outcome, you realize that you have the ability to forgive!

4. SEE THE DISADVANTAGES OF UNFORGIVENESS AND THAT WILL HELP YOU TO FORGIVE.

Then his lord, after that he had called him, said unto him, O thou wicked servant, I forgave thee all that debt, because thou desiredst me: Shouldest not thou also have had compassion on thy fellowservant, even as I had pity on thee? And his lord was wroth, AND DELIVERED HIM TO THE TORMENTORS, TILL HE SHOULD PAY ALL THAT WAS DUE UNTO HIM. So likewise shall my heavenly Father do also unto you, if ye from your hearts forgive not every one his brother their trespasses.

Matthew 18:32-35

Are there any disadvantages of unforgiveness? YES!

God will not forgive you for any of your sins, and you are not going to have any of your prayers answered if you do not forgive. The devil will torment you for your unforgiveness. Powerful men of God may lay hands on you, but the tormentors will remain in your life because of your unforgiveness.

I heard of a pastor's wife who was suffering from multiple sclerosis. She had suffered emotional hurts from within and without the church. She could not forgive those who had criticized her husband. (Sometimes it is the pastors' wives who endure a lot of ministerial hurts and pains).

When her husband travelled, God ministered to her to forgive. When she forgave those people who hurt her, she received her healing miraculously. To her husband's utter surprise, here she was, standing at the airport waiting for him when he returned from a trip. This was a wheelchair-bound woman; and there she was, free from unforgiveness and therefore free from multiple sclerosis.

The tormentors can have access to torment you with sicknesses, diseases, poverty, and marital disharmony, when you do not release those who hurt you. Could that explain your lack of breakthroughs? The price of unforgiveness is too high.

5. SEE THE ADVANTAGES OF FORGIVENESS AND THAT WILL HELP YOU TO FORGIVE.

But there is forgiveness with thee, THAT THOU MAYEST BE FEARED.

Psalm 130:4

One of the major advantages of forgiveness is that forgiveness makes you a great person! When you forgive people you will be feared! Through your ability to forgive you become a great person. Not only will your prayers be answered but you become more powerful spiritually, physically and emotionally. Forgiveness makes you a great person.

The former South African President, Nelson Mandela is considered one of the greatest men in the world - because of forgiveness. Mandela was sent to prison for twenty-seven years, by the white apartheid government. He was separated from his home, his wife and children. He spent the better part of his life in prison. This was a man, who under normal circumstances should not have forgiven his enemies. Indeed, it seems he was able to forgive his white oppressors and form a reconciliatory government with them. It is this apparent forgiveness that made him such a great person.

CHAPTER 6

Love is Forgiveness and Forgiveness is Love

Love ... does not act unbecomingly; it does not seek its own, is not provoked, DOES NOT TAKE INTO ACCOUNT A WRONG SUFFERED

1 Corinthians 13:4-5 (NASB 1995)

Forgiveness is love and love is forgiveness! Someone who loves you is someone who has forgiven you. When a couple has lived together for a long time and are still in love, it means they have forgiven each other many times. Never forget that love is forgiveness and forgiveness is love! Love is forgiveness and forgiveness is love! A loving person is a forgiving person. Someone who loves many people has forgiven many people.

Love is very important for a Christian, therefore forgiveness is very important for a Christian. Because love is very important for a Christian, forgiveness is very important for a Christian. Love goes along with forgiveness! A loving person is a forgiving person. If you want to develop your ability to love, you must develop your ability to forgive. If love is important to you, forgiveness must be important to you too.

In this chapter, we see the critical importance of love. The critical importance of love is therefore the critical importance of forgiveness. Let us see why love and forgiveness are important.

Love is Important; Therefore Forgiveness is Important

1. LOVE AND FORGIVENESS ARE IMPORTANT BECAUSE LOVE IS THE GREATEST COMMANDMENT.

Jesus said unto him, Thou shalt love the Lord thy God with all thy heart, and with all thy soul, and with all thy mind. This is the first and great commandment.

Matthew 22:37-38

If love is the greatest commandment, then forgiveness becomes the greatest commandment too. One of the greatest and most important instructions you will ever have from the

Lord is the instruction to love and forgive. There are going to be many opportunities to fulfil this all-important commandment to love and forgive.

People who will offend you are somewhere organising themselves to approach you to provoke you. Some of the people who are going to offend you are not yet born. Some of the people who will offend you are children. They are growing up and getting ready to offend you. Once you land in this world you must expect to have numerous opportunities to fulfil the greatest command ever given to mankind. Unlike the mission field that is waiting for you to come there, opportunities to be offended and hurt by someone will come to you. Love is forgiveness and forgiveness is love! A loving person is a forgiving person. Someone who loves many people has forgiven many people.

2. LOVE AND FORGIVENESS ARE IMPORTANT BECAUSE THAT IS OUR GOAL.

But THE GOAL OF OUR INSTRUCTION IS LOVE from a pure heart and a good conscience and a sincere faith.

1 Timothy 1:5 (NASB)

The goal of all the commandments and teachings we receive from God is love. Ultimately, God is trying to develop in us a new character of love. Christianity is supposed to give birth to a new person who is walking in the love and forgiveness of God. Every experience and every teaching you have had is because of love.

There are many terrible experiences that you can have in this life. There are many hurts that you can expect. There will be sad days! There will be difficult days! There will be treachery! There will be wickedness! But the goal of all these is to get you to walk in love!

3. LOVE AND FORGIVENESS ARE IMPORTANT BECAUSE THEY HELP YOU TO PASS FROM LIFE TO DEATH.

We know that we have passed from death unto life, because we love the brethren. He that loveth not his brother abideth in death.

1 John 3:14

Through love you pass from death to life. The presence of Christian love reveals that you have passed from the condition of death to the condition of life. When you do not love, you pass from life to death! When you do not forgive, you pass from life to death!

Death envelops all those who are not able to forgive. Death enters your existence when you do not forgive those who have offended you. Study this scripture carefully. It is clear that you transition from life to death because you lack love. You transition from life to death because you lack forgiveness.

4. LOVE AND FORGIVENESS ARE IMPORTANT BECAUSE THEY PREVENT YOU FROM BECOMING NOTHING.

Though I speak with the tongues of men and of angels, and have not charity, I am become as sounding brass, or a tinkling cymbal. And though I have the gift of prophecy, and understand all mysteries, and all knowledge; and though I have all faith, so that I could remove mountains, and have not charity, I AM NOTHING. And though I bestow all my goods to feed the poor, and though I give my body to be burned, and have not charity, IT PROFITETH ME NOTHING.

1 Corinthians 13:1-3

The scripture above reveals that although you speak in tongues and pray a lot but have not love and forgiveness, your prayers and tongues are simply noise before the throne of grace.

God will ask His angel to turn the volume of your prayers down. You are just a noisy gong and a tinkling cymbal when you do not live in forgiveness. Do you want all your prayers to turn into noise? If not, start forgiving and releasing the sins and errors of those who have hurt you.

Although you prophesy and preach beautifully and know a lot about God and His word, but you do not forgive, you are actually nothing. People may think of you as a great person; but in the eyes of God you are nothing because you do not forgive and love people. Love is forgiveness and forgiveness is love! A forgiving person is a loving person!

Give and it shall be given unto you, good measure, pressed down, shaken together and running over (Luke 6:38). Giving is supposed to benefit you! Giving is supposed to profit you! When you give your offerings and tithes, you open the windows of heaven and a blessing is poured out on you. However, if you do not forgive people, you lose the benefit of giving.

The scripture declares your giving "profiteth you nothing" without love. It is amazing that many Christians give tithes and offerings but do not benefit much from their giving. People think that the scriptures have failed. They say, "I gave so much to God but I have not reaped a harvest." Could this be the reason why you have not reaped a harvest? Is it possible that you are suffering from a lack of love and forgiveness? A loving person is a forgiving person! Without forgiveness, you will not benefit from your giving.

I once read a book whose title was "*It's not working, Brother John.*" In this book, John Avanzini shared twenty-five reasons why some people give tithes and offerings and still do not seem to benefit from it. Amazingly, this book clearly tells us that people do not benefit from tithes and offerings because they lack love and forgiveness.

5. LOVE AND FORGIVENESS ARE IMPORTANT TO PREVENT YOU FROM LOSING YOUR PLACE.

Unto the angel of the church of Ephesus write; These things saith he that holdeth the seven stars in his right hand, who walketh in the midst of the seven golden candlesticks; I know thy works, and thy labour, and thy patience, and how thou canst not bear them which are evil: and thou hast tried them which say they are apostles, and are not, and hast found them liars: And hast borne, and hast patience, and for my name's sake hast laboured, and hast not fainted.

Nevertheless I have somewhat against thee, because thou hast left thy first love.

Remember therefore from whence thou art fallen, and repent, and do the first works; OR ELSE I WILL COME UNTO THEE QUICKLY, AND WILL REMOVE THY CANDLESTICK OUT OF HIS PLACE, except thou repent.

Revelation 2:1-5

Working very hard is important. God notices your labour and your patience. God notices how melancholic you are and how you cannot stand evil. You have zero tolerance for evil! If you are hardworking and yet fail in the area of forgiveness, you are failing totally.

Failure to walk in love and forgiveness puts your place and position at risk. You may be standing at the forefront of the ministry today but you will be demoted and replaced if you do not forgive and walk in love.

The Lord had a very strong warning for the Ephesian church - repent from being unloving and unforgiving or I will come and remove you out of your place!

Kenneth Hagin tells a story of how he met a mighty man of God outside his evangelistic tent. As he departed, the word of the Lord came to him about this mighty man of God, "Walk in love in relation to your fellow brethren". The Lord was warning this man of God to correct himself in relation to love and forgiveness. This man of God apparently did not change that important aspect and died suddenly in the midst of his years. He was just thirty-six years old when he died.

It is important to take warnings about love and forgiveness very seriously. Your rank, your position and your place are all at risk if you do not walk in the love of God. You may do great things and speak great words but it all amounts to nothing if you do not have love and forgiveness.

6. LOVE AND FORGIVENESS ARE IMPORTANT BECAUSE THEY ARE PROOF THAT YOU LOVE GOD.

If a man say, I love God, and hateth his brother, he is a liar: for he that loveth not his brother whom he hath seen, how can he love God whom he hath not seen?

1 John 4:20

Since love is so important, we must make sure that we are walking in love. Since forgiveness is so important, we must make sure that we are walking in forgiveness.

Sometimes, it is unclear whether loving God is the same as loving people. However, loving God is very linked to loving people. How is loving people linked to loving God? Loving people is the sign that you love God! How can you claim that you love God whom you cannot see? (1 John 4:20) What about the people you can see? How do you relate to the people you can see? From today, you must remember this rule of love.

If you cannot forgive the husband whom you see, you cannot claim that you love God whom you cannot see!

If you cannot forgive the wife whom you see, you cannot claim that you love God whom you cannot see!

31

If you do not love and forgive the pastor whom you see, you cannot claim that you love the God whom you cannot see!

If you cannot forgive your friend whom you see, you cannot claim that you love God whom you cannot see!

If you cannot love and forgive your colleagues at work, whom you see, you cannot claim that you love God whom you cannot see!

If you do not love and forgive your fellow church members, whom you see, you cannot claim that you love God whom you cannot see!

7. LOVE AND FORGIVENESS ARE IMPORTANT FOR THE DAY OF JUDGMENT.

Herein is our love made perfect, that we may have BOLDNESS IN THE DAY OF JUDGMENT: because as he is, so are we in this world.

1 John 4:17

On the Day of Judgment, love will be the most important topic. In some examinations, there are compulsory questions. No matter what you do, you have to answer those questions. Why are those questions compulsory? They are compulsory because they are the most important questions that reveal whether you know the most important things.

You can have boldness in the Day of Judgment if you are strong in love and forgiveness. On the Day of Judgment, many of the great things you have accomplished may not count. Your ability to love and forgive may be the main question thrown at you on the Day of Judgment.

Do you want to be bold on the Day of Judgment or do you want to be frightened out of your wits? It is time to master the art of forgiveness made easy! It is time to specialize in walking in love and forgiveness!

32

I suggest that you read Rick Joyner's book, *The Final Quest*. In this book, you will see stories of pastors who died and went to heaven to receive their judgments. Many of these pastors had a terrible time before the judgment throne because they fell short in love and forgiveness. Some of them were famous on earth but were severely reprimanded before the judgment seat and thrown into outer darkness. Remember that outer darkness is a zone reserved for unforgiving people.

CHAPTER 7

Forgiveness Changes Your Destiny

And Joseph said unto his brethren, Come near to me, I pray you. And they came near. And he said, I am Joseph your brother, whom ye sold into Egypt. Now therefore be not grieved, nor angry with yourselves, that ye sold me hither: for God did send me before you to preserve life. For these two years hath the famine been in the land: and yet there are five years, in the which there shall neither be earing nor harvest. AND GOD SENT ME BEFORE YOU TO PRESERVE YOU A POSTERITY IN THE EARTH, AND TO SAVE YOUR LIVES BY A GREAT DELIVERANCE. So now it was not you that sent me hither, but God: and he hath made me a father to Pharaoh, and lord of all his house, and a ruler throughout all the land of Egypt.

Genesis 45:4-8

The destiny of Joseph depended on him being able to forgive his brethren. If Joseph had not been able to forgive his brethren, he would not have saved the nation of Israel. Your destiny will also depend on your being able to forgive your brethren.

1. FORGIVENESS WILL CAUSE YOU TO FULFILL YOUR DREAMS

And Joseph dreamed a dream, and he told it his brethren: and they hated him yet the more. And he said unto them, Hear, I pray you, this dream which I have dreamed:

For, behold, we were binding sheaves in the field, and, lo, my sheaf arose, and also stood upright; and, behold, your sheaves stood round about, and made obeisance to my sheaf.

And his brethren said to him, Shalt thou indeed reign over us? or shalt thou indeed have dominion over us? And they hated him yet the more for his dreams, and for his words.

Genesis 37:5-8

The legendary forgiveness of Joseph allowed him to see the fulfillment of his dreams.

Dead bodies cannot come and bow down to you. If Joseph had killed the people who sold him, he would not have lived to see his dream come to pass. His dreams needed his forgiveness to materialise!

Joseph dreamed that his family would come and bow down to him. This dream was in his heart. Perhaps, you also have dreams and visions. Your dreams and visions will come to pass when you forgive people. If Joseph had walked in revenge and hatred, he would have organized the summary execution of his brothers. How then could his executed brothers come and bow down before him. They would be dead bodies!

It is important that you forgive people so that your dreams come to pass. Look at the following scriptures to see how Joseph's dreams came to pass through forgiveness. Each time his living brethren bowed down to him, his dreams were coming to pass.

And Joseph was the governor over the land, and he it was that sold to all the people of the land: AND JOSEPH'S BRETHREN CAME, AND BOWED DOWN THEMSELVES BEFORE HIM WITH THEIR FACES TO THE EARTH.

Genesis 42:6

And when Joseph came home, THEY BROUGHT HIM THE PRESENT WHICH WAS IN THEIR HAND INTO THE HOUSE, AND BOWED THEMSELVES TO HIM TO THE EARTH.

And he asked them of their welfare, and said, Is your father well, the old man of whom ye spake? Is he yet alive?

And they answered, Thy servant our father is in good health, he is yet alive. AND THEY BOWED DOWN THEIR HEADS, AND MADE OBEISANCE.

Genesis 43:26-28

2. FORGIVENESS WILL MAKE YOU A NOURISHER OF PEOPLE.

Through forgiveness Joseph became a nourisher of people. He nourished his whole family in Goshen. How can you nourish people whom you have killed? Do not kill the people who have offended you. They may be the people through whom you become a mighty man of God and be able to nourish people.

So now it was not you that sent me hither, but God: and he hath made me a father to Pharaoh, and lord of all his house, and a ruler throughout all the land of Egypt. Haste ye, and go up to my father, and say unto him, Thus saith thy son Joseph, God hath made me lord of all Egypt: come down unto me, tarry not: AND THOU SHALT DWELL IN THE

LAND OF GOSHEN, AND THOU SHALT BE NEAR UNTO ME, THOU, AND THY CHILDREN, AND THY CHILDREN'S CHILDREN, AND THY FLOCKS, AND THY HERDS, AND ALL THAT THOU HAST: AND THERE WILL I NOURISH THEE; for yet there are five years of famine; lest thou, and thy household, and all that thou hast, come to poverty.

Genesis 45:8-11

3. FORGIVENESS WILL MAKE YOU A LEADER.

Forgiveness will make you a leader of many people. Many of the people that you will lead will be people that you have had to forgive. A leader is someone who is in charge of both good and bad people. It will never be the case that the entire congregation is full of loving, nice and good people. There will always be bad people in your team.

Through forgiveness Joseph became a leader of a large number of wicked people. Joseph's brothers were a well-known bunch of evil men who went as far as to sell their own brother. Joseph's brothers did not just attempt to sell their brother, they actually did sell him off as a slave. Joseph's brothers were liars and deceivers. They deceived their father for fifteen years. They lived a lie for fifteen long years! Joseph was one year in Potiphar's house and twelve years in the prison. Joseph revealed himself to his brothers two years after the famine started. "And there will I nourish thee; for yet there are five years of famine; lest thou, and thy household, and all that thou hast, come to poverty" (Genesis 45:11).

Anyone who is able to deceive a close relative for fifteen years, is a high-level deceiver and pretender. Jacob's sons were wicked and deceptive to their father. They were high-level deceivers because they could perfectly deceive their father for fifteen years.

They knew that they were breaking their father's heart but they did it anyway. They could have told Jacob where Joseph was. Jacob could have sent a delegation to Egypt to search for his son. But they maintained the perfect lie for fifteen good years. (Perhaps, fifteen years is the maximum time a human being can perfectly deceive another.)

Unfortunately, there was no milk of kindness in Joseph's brothers. They did not pity their father. Joseph's brothers were men of conspiracy. They were able to keep a tight secret amongst themselves for so many years. Every time they were with their father, they knew they were deceiving him. Not one of them opened their mouths to reveal the secret.

The destiny of Joseph depended on him being able to forgive these undeniably wicked, deceptive and evil men. One day, you will discover that your destiny depends on your ability to genuinely forgive men who have proved themselves to be indisputably evil. Destiny is not possible without forgiveness!

Joseph nourished his whole family in Goshen. How can you lead people that you have killed? Do not kill the people who have offended you. They may be the people through whom you become a mighty man of God.

So now it was not you that sent me hither, but God: and he hath made me a father to Pharaoh, and lord of all his house, and a ruler throughout all the land of Egypt.

Genesis 45:8

4. FORGIVENESS WILL MAKE YOU FEARED BY MEN.

AND WHEN JOSEPH'S BRETHREN SAW THAT THEIR FATHER WAS DEAD, THEY SAID, JOSEPH WILL PERADVENTURE HATE US, and will certainly requite us all the evil which we did unto him.

And they sent a messenger unto Joseph, saying, Thy father did command before he died, saying, so shall ye say unto Joseph, Forgive, I pray thee now, the trespass of thy brethren, and their sin; for they did unto thee evil: and now, we pray thee, forgive the trespass of the servants of the God of thy father. And Joseph wept when they spake unto him.

And his brethren also went and fell down before his face; and they said, Behold, we be thy servants.

AND JOSEPH SAID UNTO THEM, FEAR NOT: FOR AM I IN THE PLACE OF GOD? But as for you, ye thought evil against me; but God meant it unto good, to bring to pass, as it is this day, to save much people alive.

NOW THEREFORE FEAR YE NOT: I WILL NOURISH YOU, AND YOUR LITTLE ONES. And he comforted them, and spake kindly unto them.

Genesis 50:15-21

Even though Joseph had forgiven his brothers, they were afraid of him. Forgiveness makes you a great person. Forgiveness makes people fear you! Notice what the one hundredth and thirtieth Psalm says – "There is forgiveness with thee that thou mayest be feared."

Forgiveness imputes to you a kind of formidable power and superhuman awesomeness! Everyone expects you to strike out at your enemy and crush him when you get the opportunity. When you do not do that, it makes you an extraordinary person. Rise up and take the great advantage that forgiveness gives you in this life! Become an awesome godlike figure through your ability to forgive!

But there is forgiveness with thee, that thou mayest be feared.

Psalm 130:4

5. FORGIVENESS WILL REVERSE A NEGATIVE DESTINY.

And ye shall tell my father of all my glory in Egypt, and of all that ye have seen; and ye shall haste and bring down my father hither.

Genesis 45:13

But as for you, ye thought evil against me; but God meant it unto good, to bring to pass, as it is this day, to save much people alive.

Genesis 50:20

The scripture shows us that Joseph reversed his negative destiny through the power of forgiveness. Instead of being a prisoner and a slave, he became a father to Pharaoh and the lord to all his house.

Joseph's life was full of glory and beauty. Instead of shame and imprisonment, he was experiencing the glory of God on his life. This is going to be your story when you learn to forgive! Every negative destiny and picture of your life will be reversed! Your life will be filled with the glory of God!

6. FORGIVENESS WILL PREVENT YOU FROM BECOMING AN AVENGER AND A MURDERER.

When Joseph's brothers saw that their father was dead, they said, "WHAT IF JOSEPH BEARS A GRUDGE AGAINST US AND PAYS US BACK IN FULL FOR ALL THE WRONG WHICH WE DID TO HIM!"

So they sent a message to Joseph, saying, "Your father charged before he died, saying,

'Thus you shall say to Joseph, "Please forgive, I beg you, the transgression of your brothers and their sin, for they did you wrong."' And now, please forgive the transgression of the servants of the God of your father." And Joseph wept when they spoke to him. Then his brothers also came and fell down before him and said, "Behold, we are your servants."

But Joseph said to them, "Do not be afraid, for am I in God's place?" As for you, you meant evil against me, but God meant it for good in order to bring about this present result, to preserve many people alive.

Genesis 50:15-20 (NASB)

The sons of Jacob were expecting Joseph to pay them back for what they had done to him. They had stolen his life when he was a teenager and sold him into a life of hardship and wickedness. Joseph had been beaten many times as a slave. He had suffered at the hands of slave masters. By the time Joseph met up with his younger brother Benjamin, Benjamin had given birth to ten sons.

Benjamin had had a normal life whilst his bigger brother, Joseph, was floundering in an Egyptian jail. Joseph was a prisoner when his younger brother was giving birth to ten sons.

If Joseph was to pay his brothers back for what they had done, he would have had to take their lives just as they took his life away. Perhaps he would have had to throw them into jail and make some of them slaves too. That would have been the only fair recompense for what they had done to him. Joseph refused to become and avenger and a murderer. This will be your story too! You will never be an avenger! Neither will you turn into a killer! You will not pay back evil for evil, but you will trust in God!

7. FORGIVENESS WILL ALLOW YOU TO INHERIT GREAT THINGS.

And he blessed them that day, saying, In thee shall Israel bless, saying, God make thee as Ephraim and as Manasseh: and he set Ephraim before Manasseh. And Israel said unto Joseph, Behold, I die: but God shall be with you, and bring you again unto the land of your fathers. Moreover I have given to thee one portion above thy brethren, which I took out of the hand of the Amorite with my sword and with my bow.

Genesis 48:20-22

Forgiveness will make you have one portion above your brethren. Jacob had a good reason to give Joseph two portions of inheritance. If Joseph had killed his brothers, he would not have seen his father again. If Joseph had killed his brothers, his father Jacob would not have shared his inheritance to anyone because all his children would have been dead. You will not enjoy the inheritance God has for you if you do not learn to forgive. Begin to forgive and to let go so that you can enjoy the inheritance God has for you.

8. FORGIVENESS WILL PREVENT YOU FROM BEING ISOLATED AND SEPARATED. FORGIVENESS WILL CAUSE YOU TO HAVE A BIG FAMILY.

All the souls that came with Jacob into Egypt, which came out of his loins, besides Jacob's sons' wives, all the souls were threescore and six;

And the sons of Joseph, which were born him in Egypt, were two souls: all the souls of the house of Jacob, which came into Egypt, were threescore and ten.

Genesis 46:26-27

Forgiveness will cause you not to be isolated. Isolation and separation take place when you cannot forgive. Pastors who never forgive church members for their lapses will not have large churches. It takes a lot of forgiveness to build a large family. There is always something hurtful that happens when you interact with people.

Gradually, people who are hurt withdraw themselves from those who hurt them and live alone. Anyone with a large church and a large family has exhibited a lot of forgiveness and love. Many people live alone because they cannot forgive their fellow human beings. There are many cities in which more than fifty per cent of their inhabitants live alone.

9. FORGIVENESS WILL CAUSE YOU TO END THE CYCLE OF EVIL.

And ye shall tell my father of all my glory in Egypt, and of all that ye have seen; and ye shall haste and bring down my father hither.

And he fell upon his brother Benjamin's neck, and wept; and Benjamin wept upon his neck. Moreover he kissed all his brethren, and wept upon them: and after that his brethren talked with him.

Genesis 45:13-15

Joseph had the choice of ending the cycle of evil that began in his brothers. Evil always moves around in cycles. It is only through love and forgiveness that the cycle is broken. Joseph could have gone on to show his strength and power over his brothers. If Joseph had fought back, his brothers would have retaliated. His brothers would have claimed that he provoked them with his dreams and his rude predictions and that he deserved what he got. Evil would have continued in a never-ending cycle, as it is in most families and nations. Today, you have a chance to end the cycle of evil by walking in love and forgiveness!

CHAPTER 8

Forgiveness Allows Vengeance to Happen

Dearly beloved, avenge not yourselves, but rather give place unto wrath: for it is written, Vengeance is mine; I will repay, saith the Lord. Therefore IF THINE ENEMY HUNGER, FEED HIM; IF HE THIRST, GIVE HIM DRINK: FOR IN SO DOING THOU SHALT HEAP COALS OF FIRE ON HIS HEAD.

Romans 12:19-20

G ive place to the wrath of God! This simply means do not block God's anger. Allow God's pure anger to flow against harmful, wicked, ungrateful, deceptive and treacherous people.

It is important that you practice forgiveness. As you forgive those who have harmed you, you pour coals of fire on their head. Don't you want to pour coals of fire on the heads of those who have hurt you?

Genuine forgiveness will cause you to feed your hungry enemy and bless your thirsty foe. As you show acts of kindness and love out of forgiveness, it ignites the vengeance of God against your enemies.

God is desperate to repay your enemies for what they have done against you. The only thing that is blocking Him from unleashing His vengeance against your enemies is your unforgiveness, bitterness and personal revenge.

1. Do not be afraid to forgive people.

Do not think that your forgiveness is the end of the story! Those who have harmed you must watch out because God will pay them back. God is into repayment for evil! God will come with a vengeance! God will come with a recompense! God has a payment plan! Your duty is to forgive and God's duty is to repay!

Say to them that are of a fearful heart, be strong, fear not: behold, YOUR GOD WILL COME WITH VENGEANCE, even God with a recompence; he will come and save you.

Isaiah 35:4

2. Concentrate on forgiveness so that God can concentrate on vengeance.

God is an avenger! His Spirit and His anointing will bring about a day of vengeance from God on your behalf.

The Spirit of the Lord God is upon me; because the Lord hath anointed me to preach good tidings unto the meek; he hath sent me to bind up the brokenhearted, to proclaim liberty to the captives, and the opening of the prison to them that are bound; To proclaim the acceptable year of the Lord, and THE DAY OF VENGEANCE OF OUR GOD; to comfort all that mourn;

Isaiah 61:1-2

3. God prefers to take revenge personally.

O LORD GOD, TO WHOM VENGEANCE BELONGETH; O God, to whom vengeance belongeth, shew thyself.

Psalm 94:1

There are many films that depict sweet revenge. Most people like to watch a film that ends in sweet revenge. There is something in you that wants to avenge and wants bad people to be punished for what they have done. In a sense, that is a God aspect of you. God, however, requests that you submerge that feeling and trust Him to do the avenging part.

Vengeance is one of God's personal contributions to your life. Why would you deprive God of His vengeance on your behalf? "Vengeance is mine, says the Lord!" (Romans 12:19) Forgiveness must engage you and keep you busy. When you are busy forgiving, you will not have time to avenge yourself and take over God's work. God is far better at avenging than you! God has inventive and creative ways to avenge all wickedness that has been manifested against you.

4. Pray for vengeance.

And the Lord said, Hear what the unjust judge saith. AND SHALL NOT GOD AVENGE HIS OWN ELECT, WHICH CRY DAY AND NIGHT UNTO HIM, though he bear long with them? I tell you that he will avenge them speedily. Nevertheless when the Son of man cometh, shall he find faith on the earth?

Luke 18:6-8

Praying for vengeance is a good prayer topic. It is a topic taught by Jesus Christ Himself. Praying for vengeance puts the job of avenging squarely in the hands of God.

Concentrate on forgiveness and pray to God to carry out His role of avenging you. When Jesus taught on prayer, He explained that God wanted to avenge you speedily. God is an avenger! Jesus taught us to leave the vengeance to God.

Indeed, Jesus taught us to pray night and day and that God would avenge us. Jesus did not only teach that you should forgive. He also taught that you should pray for vengeance. These two things go together: genuine forgiveness and the prayer for God to avenge you. Both of these principles were taught by Jesus and both are true. The mystery of God's vengeance is that it is blocked by your interference.

5. God has a repayment plan for all your enemies.

Know therefore that the LORD thy God, he is God, the faithful God, which keepeth covenant and mercy with them that love him and keep his commandments to a thousand generations; AND REPAYETH THEM THAT HATE HIM TO THEIR FACE, TO DESTROY THEM: HE WILL NOT BE SLACK TO HIM THAT HATETH HIM, HE WILL REPAY HIM TO HIS FACE.

Deuteronomy 7:9-10

God has a plan to repay everyone who has been nasty to you. Do not worry about it at all. God will pay them better than you can. God repays those who hate Him. God is into repayments! He will take up your repayments as well!

This is why the scripture warns against paying back yourself. "Do not take your own revenge!" That is God's commandment to you! Give place for the wrath of God to be revealed in your life. (Romans 12:19)

As long as you live in bitterness, hatred and revenge, God will not have the place that He needs to take vengeance on your behalf. God has a repayment plan for all those who harm you. He has promised to pay them back. "I will repay them" is what He says.

Conclusion

It is my prayer that you will be delivered from the snare of unforgiveness. Unforgiveness is a cloud of evil that has settled on most Christians. Do not allow yourself to fall into the complicated evils that befall those who refuse to walk in love and forgiveness. Pray for the grace to forgive! Pray for a loving, forgiving and sweet spirit! God has determined to help you to walk in His love.

To the writing of many letters and the making of many books there is no end. With these few words, console and comfort yourself in the Lord.